My Own Digital Art Paintings: Diamond Cube.

Frank Benson:

Claude Monet: River Seine.

Diamond Art:

Van Gogh: Daffodils:

Cezanne: Eiffel Tower.

Chinese Oriental Art:

Van Gogh: Lotus Flower.

Pablo Picasso:

Claude Monet: Butterfly.

Claude Monet (contd).

Vincent Van Gogh:

Van Gogh: Tuscany.

Above: Zion National Park, USA.

Heavy Paintwork (no particular style):

(Original Art: Matterhorn, Switzerland)

Diamond Art (with different lighting):

(Gold Sphere, Diamond Prism, Silver Sphere).

My Abstract Art (simulating Palette Knife):

www.ingramcontent.com/pod-product-compliance
Lightning Source LLC
Chambersburg PA
CBHW050912180526
45159CB00007B/2892